pray the
scriptures

pray the
scriptures

A 40-Day Prayer Experience

Kevin Johnson

BETHANYHOUSE
a division of Baker Publishing Group
Minneapolis, Minnesota

© 2013 by Kevin Johnson

Published by Bethany House Publishers
11400 Hampshire Avenue South
Bloomington, Minnesota 55438
www.bethanyhouse.com

Bethany House Publishers is a division of
Baker Publishing Group, Grand Rapids, Michigan

Printed in the United States of America

Library of Congress Cataloging-in-Publication Data
Johnson, Kevin (Kevin Walter)
    Pray the scriptures : a 40-day prayer experience / Kevin Johnson.
      pages cm
      Summary: "A unique 40-day prayer experience guides readers in the discipline of praying God's own words back to him"—Provided by publisher.
      ISBN 978-0-7642-1103-4 (pbk. : alk. paper)
      1. Prayer—Christianity. I. Title.
    BV210.3.J64 2013
    242'.722—dc23   2013002248

Cover design by Dan Pitts

13   14   15   16   17   18   19   7   6   5   4   3   2   1

To the people of Emmaus Road Church
as we walk in the way together

Contents

Contents

Introduction

Back in the earliest days of the New Testament church, Peter and John had the unfortunate experience of being caught doing good. These close friends and followers of Jesus were heading to the temple to pray when they were confronted by a man unable to walk since birth. When he asked for money, they had nothing to give. But they commanded him in the name of Jesus to rise up and walk. The man stood, then went "walking and jumping, and praising God" (Acts 3:8 NIV).

The amazement of the crowds upset the ruling religious leaders, who seized Peter and John and tossed them in jail. Once on trial, these two men pointed out that they were being bullied for the crime of kindness. Dumbfounded, the court officials released them, ordering them to never again mention Jesus.

Peter and John immediately returned to their friends and repeated everything the chief priests and other leaders had told them. After hearing these details, the followers of Jesus prayed loudly together (Acts 4:23–24). Their words formed as an instant and instinctive response to the press of real circumstances.

Their prayer started with worship. "Sovereign Lord . . . you made the heavens and the earth and the sea, and everything in them" (Acts 4:24 NIV). Opening with "Sovereign Lord" was like saying "O God, who is in charge of everything" or "O God, the ruler of all." To say "You made the heavens and the earth" means "You made everything there is—nothing exists that didn't come from you."

And then they prayed, "You made the sea." We might read that as "God, you created the beach and sunshine." Or "You made that oceanside place where I want to retire and feel the sand between my toes." But the Hebrews didn't have happy feelings about large bodies of water. The sea meant chaos. They were saying, "God, you are master of chaos and everything we can't control," which fits the outrageous scene of Peter and John being arrested and thrown in jail for doing kindness in the name of Christ. All of this adds up to saying, "God, you're in charge. You're in control of this situation we're in."

Then these early Christians did an intriguing thing. They prayed the Scriptures, quoting Psalm 2:1–2 to God. What they said amounts to "You told us a long time ago that people would oppose Jesus." They prayed, "You spoke long ago by the Holy Spirit through our ancestor David, your servant, saying, 'Why were the nations so angry? Why did they waste their time with futile plans? The kings of the earth prepared for battle; the rulers gathered together against the Lord and against his Messiah'" (Acts 4:25–26 NLT).

Praying Scripture

All of Scripture can teach us to pray. I wrote *Pray the Scriptures Bible* as an outflow of ministry and life. The idea began as a simple act of pairing Bible verses and prayer on posters for people to wander around and ponder during worship. That exercise reflected my own habit of a moment-by-moment conversation with God, especially when studying Scripture. As a follower of Jesus, spiritual leader, and author determined to make the Bible real and relevant to all ages, I developed an unconscious pattern of responding in prayer to passages I studied. Because God spoke to me, I spoke back to him.

As a next step to *Pray the Scriptures Bible*, this book will help you build your own habit of praying Scripture by leading you to respond to forty daily Bible readings. There are passages reminding you of God's unstoppable love and his plan to lift you to new life. Others help you express a craving for God. Some lay down practical challenges for you to obey. Others let you track with Jesus as he moves from his garden agony to the cross and resurrection and beyond.

For each passage I provide an opening thought. I finish with questions to answer on your own or with others. In the middle I split up the Bible passage and offer words and short phrases to prompt you to pray Scripture back to God. Feel free to use these prompts or to respond with your own thoughts. Dare to share your prayers with others, and listen to what they said to God. There are themes that weave from one day to the next, but you can also move through the readings in whatever order you choose. Groups studying this book can work through it at any comfortable pace.

Throughout this book you will engage in an uncomplicated response to God's words. Many passages move you to *declare* who God is or what he has done, is doing, or will do. You *identify* with a thought or feeling. That might prompt you to *confess* something that's come between you and God or to *commit* to living differently. Or you might *ask* the Lord to work in you or meet a need.

My prayer is that by the end of this book you will have grown in your own one-on-one conversation with God by using Scripture as the ultimate guide to prayer—a way to process your own life circumstances and give voice to your own spiritual longings, wonderings, and worship.

Kevin Johnson
kevinjohnsonbooks.com

Jesus Your Shepherd

Picture yourself as a sheep ceasing your struggle, finding rest cradled in the arms of your shepherd. The shepherd satisfies your hunger and thirst (Psalm 23:1–2) and rescues you from lost and wounded places (Ezekiel 34:15–16). He prizes you like no other. He is wholly unlike thieves who harm you secretly . . . robbers who attack you openly . . . hired hands who abandon you when trouble nears. The shepherd gives you a name, and you follow his unique call. You scatter at the voice of an imposter. Moment by moment, the shepherd walks ahead of you, guiding you to lush pasture and guarding you from danger even at the price of his own life. As you pray John 10, discover what Jesus wants to teach you about himself—and about you.

John 10:2–5 GW

[Jesus said,] "The one who enters through the gate is the shepherd. The gatekeeper opens the gate for him, and the sheep respond to his voice. He calls his sheep by name and leads them out of the pen. After he has brought out all his sheep, he walks ahead of them. The sheep follow him because they recognize his voice. They won't follow a stranger. Instead, they will run away from a stranger because they don't recognize his voice."

Jesus, you are my shepherd. You . . .

lead me through the unknown. Father, I pray that you would take my hand and lead me through this day, this week.

Jesus, I am your sheep. I . . .

Will follow you. Show me your strength, your word, that I would lean on you.

John 10:7–10 GW

Jesus emphasized, "I can guarantee this truth: I am the gate for the sheep. All who came before I did were thieves or robbers. However, the sheep didn't respond to them. I am the gate. Those who enter the sheep pen through me will be saved. They will go in and out of the sheep pen and find food. A thief comes to steal, kill, and destroy. But I came so that my sheep will have life and so that they will have everything they need."

So many people live like thieves and robbers. They . . .

go through life hurting others. father give me strength to overcome their hurt. Help me to love you more, and love me more.

You came to . . .

to give me life. Teach me, hold me, strengthen me, to see, feel, and hear you every minute of my day. ♡

John 10:11–14 GW

"I am the good shepherd. The good shepherd gives his life for the sheep. A hired hand isn't a shepherd and doesn't own the sheep. When he sees a wolf coming, he abandons the sheep and quickly runs away. So the wolf drags the sheep away and scatters the flock. The hired hand is concerned about what he's going to get paid and not about the sheep. I am the good shepherd."

You are the good shepherd. You . . .

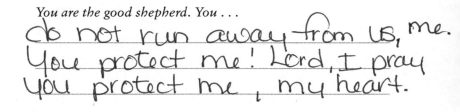

do not run away from us, me. You protect me! Lord, I pray you protect me, my heart.

Some people act like hired hands. They . . .

are not concerned about my life. Father, you love me, you want whats best for me. Thank you! I love you, Lord!

Reflect + Pray + Discuss

1. As a sheep—what do you fear? As a sheep—what do you need from Jesus your shepherd?

2. How have people acted toward you like thieves or robbers or hired hands? How is Jesus so much more than those people?

3. What kind of life does Jesus long to give you? What do you think that life looks like?

April 29, 2014

God's Welcome

God invites you to come close. Even when you feel infinitely distant from the Lord, you have an open invitation to enter his presence. On your own you are unable to approach God (Hebrews 1:3), but the death of Jesus on the cross permanently opened a new way. Jesus purifies your sins and washes away your failings, making you fit to stand in the holy presence of the King of the universe, confident that you are welcome both to worship and to ask for what you need. Entering boldly doesn't mean approaching the all-powerful God brashly or with impatient demands that he bend to your will. Honor him. Feel awe at being near him. And remember that you live in his presence even when you aren't praying. As you pray Hebrews 10, enjoy being close to your Lord.

Hebrews 10:19–20 NIV

Therefore, brothers and sisters, since we have confidence to enter the Most Holy Place by the blood of Jesus, by a

new and living way opened for us through the curtain,
that is, his body . . .

I'm sometimes afraid to come to you because . . .

I wait so long. I need to
be constantly in prayer with
you. Father help me to come
to you more.

The death of Jesus . . .

Erased all my sin. Give
me strength through your
word to fully understand and
to remind me of your everlasting
love.

Hebrews 10:21–23 NIV

. . . and since we have a great priest over the house of God,
let us draw near to God with a sincere heart and with the
full assurance that faith brings, having our hearts sprinkled
to cleanse us from a guilty conscience and having our
bodies washed with pure water. Let us hold unswervingly
to the hope we profess, for he who promised is faithful.

I'm confident to enter your holy presence because . . .

You have made me new. You
give me hope, hope that
I can rest in you.

Since you are faithful, I won't give up hope that . . .

you will ever leave me.

Hebrews 10:24–25 NIV

And let us consider how we may spur one another on toward love and good deeds, not giving up meeting together, as some are in the habit of doing, but encouraging one another—and all the more as you see the Day approaching.

I need your followers to help me . . .

be strong, to help me want to be with them. To encourage me, not to always speak of themselves. I need to know I can share with them.

Inspire and empower my spiritual friendships with . . .

your word, your love.

Reflect + Pray + Discuss

1. What keeps you from approaching God confidently?

2. How does Jesus break down those barriers?

3. Who encourages you to enjoy closeness with God and do good? How can you deepen those relationships?

April 30, 2014

Divine Streams

God promises to refresh you as you rely on him. The prophet Jeremiah described a nation that had abandoned their God, a rebellion that was "engraved with a diamond point on their stony hearts" (Jeremiah 17:1 NLT). People looked to imaginary gods, and their children witnessed their unfaithfulness. Families were in danger of losing their homes and being handed over to their enemies (17:2–5). But God declared that those who trust in him—who lean into him and put full confidence in his care—will be like trees planted by a stream. You may be surrounded by a barren wilderness, but as you send your roots into God's flowing waters, you will never fear its heat. As you pray Jeremiah 17, remind the Lord that you count on him. Look to him to keep you perpetually fruitful.

Jeremiah 17:5–6 NLT

This is what the Lord says: "Cursed are those who put their trust in mere humans, who rely on human strength and turn their hearts away from the Lord. They are like stunted shrubs in the desert, with no hope for the future. They will live in the barren wilderness, in an uninhabited salty land."

I come away disappointed when I trust in others or in my own abilities more than in you. I end up . . .

Disappointed, feeling alone and not wanting to talk to anyone. Father please forgive me for not trusting you more open my eyes, my ears and

I feel stunted and hopeless when . . . my heart to you.

When I share what I'm feeling with others, and not you. I want and need to come to you MORE.

Jeremiah 17:7–8 NLT

"But blessed are those who trust in the Lord and have made the Lord their hope and confidence. They are like trees planted along a riverbank, with roots that reach deep into the water. Such trees are not bothered by the heat or worried by long months of drought. Their leaves stay green, and they never stop producing fruit."

You give me hope and restore my confidence. I count on you to . . .

lift me up out of life's turbulence. Thank you, Lord.

I want my roots to reach deep into your waters. Teach me how to . . .

Dive more into your word, and to use your words all the time. Help me to focus more on you than my needs.

Jeremiah 17:9–10 NLT

"The human heart is the most deceitful of all things, and desperately wicked. Who really knows how bad it is? But I, the Lord, search all hearts and examine secret motives. I give all people their due rewards, according to what their actions deserve."

Show me where I deceive myself. I need to know your truth about . . .

what you would have me to do.

Search my heart. Examine my motives toward . . .

toward those who don't
care, to those who use
me.

Reflect + Pray + Discuss

1. When has relying on mere people—maybe on your-self—taken you away from God?

2. When have you faced heat or felt long droughts? How has turning to God refreshed you? How has his care prevented you from looking to false gods for help?

3. What does it look like for you to stay green and keep producing fruit? What do you need from God to thrive?

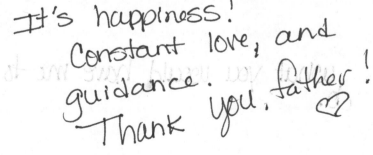

It's happiness!
Constant love, and
guidance.
Thank you, father!

God's Plan

The God you approach in prayer has a plan for your life. You might assume that his plan consists of guidance for life's details and major decisions, and the Lord does eagerly offer that wisdom (James 1:5). But his all-encompassing goal is to make you like his Son (Romans 8:29; 2 Corinthians 3:18). The faithfulness and character of Jesus illustrate what he destines you to become. But your transformation takes place in a world choked with pain. You might feel the agony of tragedy . . . inner struggles . . . hard work. All are occasions for God to display his handiwork. You can be certain that no matter what difficulties you face, God will finish what he starts in you (Philippians 1:6). As you pray Romans 8, look forward to what God is going to do in and through you.

Romans 8:22–23 MSG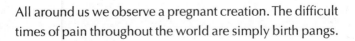

All around us we observe a pregnant creation. The difficult times of pain throughout the world are simply birth pangs.

But it's not only around us; it's *within* us. The Spirit of God is arousing us within. We're also feeling the birth pangs. These sterile and barren bodies of ours are yearning for full deliverance.

The pain I feel inside and out signals your new work. You . . .

I need deliverance from . . .

Romans 8:24–25 MSG

That is why waiting does not diminish us, any more than waiting diminishes a pregnant mother. We are enlarged in the waiting. We, of course, don't see what is enlarging us. But the longer we wait, the larger we become, and the more joyful our expectancy.

Waiting does not diminish me. It . . .

As I wait, I look forward to . . .

_____

_____

_____

Romans 8:26–28 MSG

Meanwhile, the moment we get tired in the waiting, God's Spirit is right alongside helping us along. If we don't know how or what to pray, it doesn't matter. He does our praying in and for us, making prayer out of our wordless sighs, our aching groans. He knows us far better than we know ourselves, knows our pregnant condition, and keeps us present before God. That's why we can be so sure that every detail in our lives of love for God is worked into something good.

You come alongside me when I tire. I don't know how to pray about . . .

_____

_____

_____

Your love works every detail of my life into something good. Please . . .

_____

_____

_____

Romans 8:29–30 MSG

God knew what he was doing from the very beginning. He decided from the outset to shape the lives of those who love him along the same lines as the life of his Son. The Son stands first in the line of humanity he restored. We see the original and intended shape of our lives there in him. After God made that decision of what his children should be like, he followed it up by calling people by name. After he called them by name, he set them on a solid basis with himself. And then, after getting them established, he stayed with them to the end, gloriously completing what he had begun.

Reshape my life along the lines of your Son. Give me hope that . . .

_____

_____

_____

_____

Stay with me to the end. Don't stop . . .

_____

_____

_____

_____

Reflect + Pray + Discuss

1. When have you seen God work difficulties into something good? How do you feel about that now?

2. What transformations do you see God undertaking in you right now? What changes do you fear?

3. What do you expect to look like when God is finished with you?

Unstoppable Love

When voices around you seethe with hatred, God speaks love. Even on your best days you might face adversaries and adversities. Some come in the form of external circumstances like trouble or need or persecution (John 16:33). Others are human opponents—some strangers, others with faces you know all too well (Luke 6:22). Still others are unseen supernatural forces you may never fully perceive (1 Peter 5:8). These foes kill hope. They condemn you. They conspire to discourage you and distance you from God. Worst of all, they can leave you doubting if your Lord truly cares. But God declares that none of these things or anything else in all creation can ever separate you from his love. As you pray Romans 8, rest in the truth that nothing can stop his love for you.

Romans 8:31–34 NIV

What, then, shall we say in response to these things? If God is for us, who can be against us? He who did not spare his own Son, but gave him up for us all—how will he not also, along with him, graciously give us all things? Who will bring any charge against those whom God has chosen? It is God who justifies. Who then is the one who condemns? No one. Christ Jesus who died—more than that, who was raised to life—is at the right hand of God and is also interceding for us.

Your Son is proof that . . .

_____

_____

_____

When people condemn me . . .

_____

_____

_____

Romans 8:35–36 NIV

Who shall separate us from the love of Christ? Shall trouble or hardship or persecution or famine or nakedness or danger or sword? As it is written: "For your sake we face death all day long; we are considered as sheep to be slaughtered."

I feel distant from you when . . .

_____

_____

_____

_____

Because I follow you, I face . . .

_____

_____

_____

_____

Romans 8:37–39 NIV

No, in all these things we are more than conquerors through him who loved us. For I am convinced that neither death nor life, neither angels nor demons, neither the present nor the future, nor any powers, neither height nor depth, nor anything else in all creation, will be able to separate us from the love of God that is in Christ Jesus our Lord.

Nothing can stop your love for me. Not even . . .

_____

_____

_____

_____

Your love . . .

_____

_____

_____

Reflect + Pray + Discuss

1. How do you recover when you feel cut off from God's love?

2. What future difficulties threaten to strain your relationship with God? How can you prepare for that?

3. Who in your world needs to be reminded of God's unstoppable love?

6

Ephesians 2

Lifted to Life

The truth that Jesus brings you back into relationship with God can become so familiar that it ceases to amaze. But if you forget the reality of your spiritual deadness apart from Jesus, you will inevitably fail to celebrate the good news that God has made you alive (Luke 7:47). Make it a habit of revisiting the truth that sin distances you from God. We all fall short of his glorious standard (Romans 3:23), and the result of wrongdoing is death (6:23). But God mercifully rescues you and raises you to life. He made you right with himself when you trusted that Jesus is all that he claimed to be (Ephesians 2:8). As you pray Ephesians 2, recall who you are without Jesus—and thank him for lifting you to life.

Ephesians 2:1–3 ESV

> And you were dead in the trespasses and sins in which you once walked, following the course of this world, following the prince of the power of the air, the spirit that is

now at work in the sons of disobedience—among whom we all once lived in the passions of our flesh, carrying out the desires of the body and the mind, and were by nature children of wrath, like the rest of mankind.

I once . . .

As a guilty human being, I . . .

Ephesians 2:4–7 ESV

But God, being rich in mercy, because of the great love with which he loved us, even when we were dead in our trespasses, made us alive together with Christ—by grace you have been saved—and raised us up with him and seated us with him in the heavenly places in Christ Jesus, so that in the coming ages he might show the immeasurable riches of his grace in kindness toward us in Christ Jesus.

You're rich in mercy. You . . .

_____

_____

_____

You gave me a seat with Jesus so that . . .

_____

_____

_____

Ephesians 2:8–10 ESV

For by grace you have been saved through faith. And this is not your own doing; it is the gift of God, not a result of works, so that no one may boast. For we are his workmanship, created in Christ Jesus for good works, which God prepared beforehand, that we should walk in them.

You saved me . . .

_____

_____

_____

Because I am your workmanship . . .

_____

_____

_____

Reflect + Pray + Discuss

1. What evidence do you see that God lifted you to new life?

2. How do you give credit to God for what he has done for you?

3. What good things do you think God has called you to do?

Getting Forgiveness

Your connection with God is maintained in part by your owning up to the wrong you do. If you claim to never sin, you fool only yourself. All people do evil in thoughts, words, and actions. We do bad things and neglect to do good. And just as wrongdoing strains even the strongest human friendships, disregarding God's commands creates a miserable tension between you and your Lord. Any lack of honesty compounds whatever you did wrong. But coming to God with an authentic confession and receiving his forgiveness restores your relationship to what it was at the start—your heart is unbound, your confidence restored, and your conversation can again flow freely. As you pray 1 John 1, admit your need for forgiveness and open yourself to God's mercy.

1 John 1:5–7 NCV

Here is the message we have heard from Christ and now announce to you: God is light, and in him there is no darkness at all. So if we say we have fellowship with God, but we continue living in darkness, we are liars and do not follow the truth. But if we live in the light, as God is in the light, we can share fellowship with each other. Then the blood of Jesus, God's Son, cleanses us from every sin.

You are . . .

_____

_____

_____

_____

Living in darkness . . .

_____

_____

_____

_____

1 John 1:8–10 NCV

If we say we have no sin, we are fooling ourselves, and the truth is not in us. But if we confess our sins, he will forgive our sins, because we can trust God to do what is right. He will cleanse us from all the wrongs we have done. If we say we have not sinned, we make God a liar, and we do not accept God's teaching.

If I claim I never sin . . .

I need your cleansing from . . .

-----

1 John 2:1–2 NCV

My dear children, I write this letter to you so you will not sin. But if anyone does sin, we have a helper in the presence of the Father—Jesus Christ, the One who does what is right. He died in our place to take away our sins, and not only our sins but the sins of all people.

I want to break out of my patterns of sin. Help me . . .

Thank you for . . .

Reflect + Pray + Discuss

1. When have you thought you could do wrong without damaging your relationship with God?

2. How does this passage challenge how you think and feel about forgiveness?

3. What steps can you take to create a consistent habit of honest confession?

Second Chances

The prophet Jeremiah's words that the Lord has a plan "to prosper you and not to harm you, plans to give you hope and a future" (Jeremiah 29:11 NIV) are often disconnected from their original setting. They were spoken to God's exiles, people on the edge of extinction, inhabitants of Jerusalem and Judah defeated by the Babylonians as a consequence of their sin and taken as prisoners to a distant land (2 Kings 25:1–21). They wailed bitterly at their fate (Psalm 37). False prophets assured them they would soon return home, but God told them to settle in and trust in his care. While the Lord guaranteed these promises to a special set of captives, they speak to all who need a fresh start. As you pray Jeremiah 29, remember that God never abandons his own.

Jeremiah 29:4–7 MSG

> This is the Message from God-of-the-Angel-Armies, Is-rael's God, to all the exiles I've taken from Jerusalem to

Babylon: "Build houses and make yourselves at home. Put in gardens and eat what grows in that country. Marry and have children. Encourage your children to marry and have children so that you'll thrive in that country and not waste away. Make yourselves at home there and work for the country's welfare. Pray for Babylon's well-being. If things go well for Babylon, things will go well for you."

Show me when to put down roots in a place I don't want to be. I need you to clarify . . .

How can I thrive in a miserable place? Help me to . . .

Jeremiah 29:8–9 MSG

Yes. Believe it or not, this is the Message from God-of-the-Angel-Armies, Israel's God: "Don't let all those so-called preachers and know-it-alls who are all over the place there take you in with their lies. Don't pay any attention to the fantasies they keep coming up with to please you. They're a bunch of liars preaching lies—and claiming I sent them! I never sent them, believe me." God's Decree!

Teach me to tell the difference between truth and lies about . . .

_____

_____

_____

_____

Free me from my own ideas about what is best for me. Let me dream your dreams about . . .

_____

_____

_____

_____

Jeremiah 29:10–13 MSG

This is God's Word on the subject: "As soon as Babylon's seventy years are up and not a day before, I'll show up and take care of you as I promised and bring you back home. I know what I'm doing. I have it all planned out—plans to take care of you, not abandon you, plans to give you the future you hope for. When you call on me, when you come and pray to me, I'll listen. When you come looking for me, you'll find me. Yes, when you get serious about finding me and want it more than anything else, I'll make sure you won't be disappointed."

Your plans for me are . . .

_____

_____

_____

_____

I want you more than anything else. I . . .

_____

_____

_____

_____

Reflect + Pray + Discuss

1. What kind of plans does God have for you?

2. When have you searched hard for God—and found him? When have you felt unsatisfied?

3. How do you trust God when you can't see past your current situation?

Thriving in Trials

God doesn't rush in to life's difficulties and say, "Everything is going to be all right." Sometimes everything doesn't turn out okay, at least from a human perspective. While God will at times rescue you by fixing a tough situation, his pattern throughout the Bible shows him more often letting his followers experience trials as a means of strengthening their trust in him. You may wish God would come up with a better program, but in everything he reminds you that perfect peace is a ways off (John 14:1–4; Revelation 21:3–4). Yet his power will guard you as you press on and demonstrate that your faith in him is real. As you pray 1 Peter 1, know that whatever testing you face will cause you to grow—and bring God glory.

1 Peter 1:3–5 NIV

Praise be to the God and Father of our Lord Jesus Christ! In his great mercy he has given us new birth into a living hope through the resurrection of Jesus Christ from the dead, and into an inheritance that can never perish, spoil or fade. This inheritance is kept in heaven for you, who through faith are shielded by God's power until the coming of the salvation that is ready to be revealed in the last time.

I praise you because . . .

_____

_____

_____

You shield me . . .

_____

_____

_____

1 Peter 1:6–7 NIV

In all this you greatly rejoice, though now for a little while you may have had to suffer grief in all kinds of trials. These have come so that the proven genuineness of your faith—of greater worth than gold, which perishes even though refined by fire—may result in praise, glory and honor when Jesus Christ is revealed.

I face . . .

_____

_____

_____

I trust you to . . .

_____

_____

_____

_____

1 Peter 1:8–9 NIV

Though you have not seen him, you love him; and even though you do not see him now, you believe in him and are filled with an inexpressible and glorious joy, for you are receiving the end result of your faith, the salvation of your souls.

I can't see you, but . . .

_____

_____

_____

_____

Trusting in you . . .

_____

_____

_____

_____

Reflect + Pray + Discuss

1. How do you typically react to "all kinds of trials"?

2. How do you want to alter your usual thoughts, feelings, and actions in light of God's promises?

3. Why trust God when you suffer?

Tripping Into Sin

Psalm 1 pictures a slide into evil. It starts with listening to the suggestions of evildoers . . . then going where sinners go . . . and finally joining in sinful acts. But this song from the hymnal of God's Old Testament people also illustrates a better choice. No one has to go down the road toward evil. By listening to God's teachings and thinking them through until your whole self surrenders to their truth, you will find yourself refreshed by God. But people who chase evil will find that God catches up with them. As you pray Psalm 1, tell God your plan to run toward him.

Psalm 1:1–3 NCV

> Happy are those who don't listen to the wicked, who don't go where sinners go, who don't do what evil people do. They love the Lord's teachings, and they think about those teachings day and night. They are strong, like a tree planted

by a river. The tree produces fruit in season, and its leaves don't die. Everything they do will succeed.

Alert me when I'm getting pulled into sin. I'm weak when it comes to . . .

_____

_____

_____

Your teachings . . .

_____

_____

_____

Psalm 1:4–6 NCV

But wicked people are not like that. They are like chaff that the wind blows away. So the wicked will not escape God's punishment. Sinners will not worship with God's people. This is because the Lord takes care of his people, but the wicked will be destroyed.

Don't blow me away with the wicked. Please . . .

_____

_____

_____

I'll prove my worship by . . .

Reflect + Pray + Discuss

1. Do you accept the main point of this song—that obedient people find life, and people who persist in evil are headed to destruction? Why—or why not?

2. How does God help you resist evil?

3. Where do you feel most vulnerable to temptation? What are you doing about that?

Love God, Love People

The religious leaders who confronted Jesus weren't looking for a pleasant spiritual conversation. He had just evaded a trap by the Sadducees, who aimed to draw attention to what they regarded as the absurdity of eternal life (Matthew 22:23–33). Next the Pharisees approached with their own trick question, asking Jesus to identify the law's most important command. Knowing that his questioners cared more about debating religious trivia than living out what matters most, Jesus replied that God wants to be loved with nothing less than an all-embracing passion that wells up from the interior of a person's whole being. And the Lord expects his followers to extend to people almost the same degree of un-self-centered love. As you pray Matthew 22, consider how you can expand your love for God and people.

Matthew 22:34–36 NKJV

> But when the Pharisees heard that He had silenced the Sadducees, they gathered together. Then one of them, a

lawyer, asked Him a question, testing Him, and saying, "Teacher, which is the great commandment in the law?"

I admit that I test you when I . . .

_____

_____

_____

_____

Forgive me when I trivialize your commands about . . .

_____

_____

_____

_____

Matthew 22:37–38 NKJV

Jesus said to him, "'You shall love the Lord your God with all your heart, with all your soul, and with all your mind.' This is the first and great commandment."

It's obvious I don't fully love you when I . . .

_____

_____

_____

_____

I want to put you first in my life by . . .

Matthew 22:39–40 NKJV

"And the second is like it: 'You shall love your neighbor as yourself.' On these two commandments hang all the Law and the Prophets."

I struggle to love . . .

I need your help to . . .

Reflect + Pray + Discuss

1. What priorities compete for your total devotion to God?

2. How do the demands of looking after your own needs mesh with Jesus' command to love others almost as much as you love him?

3. Where do you get power to live out these highest commands of Jesus?

The Way

When Jesus told his followers that he was the way to heaven, he sought to reassure their troubled hearts. Note that he didn't speak these famous words on a sunlit hillside, with his disciples relaxing around him and basking in his wisdom. Only hours from the cross, Jesus uttered this profound truth in the dark chaos following his predictions that one friend would betray him (John 13:21–30) and another would deny him (John 13:31–38). In your own shadowed days, you can hold to your Lord's words that he is preparing a place for you in heaven, and that he himself will lead you home. As you pray John 14, say thanks that you spend every day from now until eternity close to him.

John 14:1–3 ESV

> "Let not your hearts be troubled. Believe in God; believe also in me. In my Father's house are many rooms. If it were not so, would I have told you that I go to prepare a

place for you? And if I go and prepare a place for you, I will come again and will take you to myself, that where I am you may be also."

I'm troubled whenever I feel distant from you. I . . .

I want to be sure about my home with you. Teach me the facts about . . .

John 14:4–7 ESV

"And you know the way to where I am going." Thomas said to him, "Lord, we do not know where you are going. How can we know the way?" Jesus said to him, "I am the way, and the truth, and the life. No one comes to the Father except through me. If you had known me, you would have known my Father also. From now on you do know him and have seen him."

Because you are the way, truth, and life . . .

_____

_____

_____

I have family and friends who aren't following you home to heaven. Show yourself to . . .

_____

_____

_____

John 14:8–11 ESV

Philip said to him, "Lord, show us the Father, and it is enough for us." Jesus said to him, "Have I been with you so long, and you still do not know me, Philip? Whoever has seen me has seen the Father. How can you say, 'Show us the Father'? Do you not believe that I am in the Father and the Father is in me? The words that I say to you I do not speak on my own authority, but the Father who dwells in me does his works. Believe me that I am in the Father and the Father is in me, or else believe on account of the works themselves."

Because you came to earth and showed yourself . . .

_____

_____

_____

I rely on your promise because . . .

_____

_____

_____

_____

Reflect + Pray + Discuss

1. What convinces you that your home in heaven is real?

2. What do you expect heaven to be like? How have you reached those conclusions?

3. Who around you needs to know that Jesus is the way, truth, and life—and what part can you play in pointing them home?

13

Psalm 63

Thirst for God

God took the first steps to show you love. He created you as an object of his affection, knowing and loving you even before you were conceived (Psalm 139:13–16; Jeremiah 31:3). He reached out to you even after you turned from him (Romans 5:8). But as passionately as the Lord pursues you, he nevertheless expects you to engage in pursuing him. He promises, for example, to be found by you when you wholeheartedly search for him (Jeremiah 29:13). He encourages you to ask, seek, and knock (Matthew 7:7). And he shouts that the thirsty should come to him (John 7:37–38). God never pours water down the throats of people who don't want what he offers. But as you pray Psalm 63, be assured that he will always quench your spiritual thirst.

Psalm 63:1–2 GW

> O God, you are my God. At dawn I search for you. My soul thirsts for you. My body longs for you in a dry, parched

61

land where there is no water. So I look for you in the holy place to see your power and your glory.

I thirst for you . . .

I long to see . . .

Psalm 63:3–5 GW

My lips will praise you because your mercy is better than life itself. So I will thank you as long as I live. I will lift up my hands to pray in your name. You satisfy my soul with the richest foods. My mouth will sing your praise with joyful lips.

You deserve praise for . . .

When I worship you I feel . . .

_____

_____

_____

_____

Psalm 63:6–8 GW

As I lie on my bed, I remember you. Through the long hours of the night, I think about you. You have been my help. In the shadow of your wings, I sing joyfully. My soul clings to you. Your right hand supports me.

Day after day you . . .

_____

_____

_____

_____

When I'm close to you I can't help but . . .

_____

_____

_____

_____

Reflect + Pray + Discuss

1. What helps you speak praise aloud to God? What gets in the way?

2. At what point in your life have you most wanted to know God? Why?

3. How are you passionately seeking God right now?

Preparing for Worship

As Old Testament worshipers made their spiritual journey to Jerusalem, they sang in anticipation of meeting God. Their "Songs of Ascent" (Psalms 120–134) prepared their hearts as they made an often arduous trip from Israel's countryside to the temple. Many of their songs expressed joy. As David wrote in Psalm 122, "I rejoiced with those who said to me, 'Let us go to the house of the Lord'" (v. 1 NIV). All of these songs voiced hope in the powerful reign of the Lord of all. Psalm 121 pictures a traveler seeing the hills of the holy city and exclaiming, "Where do I get help?" The question has an obvious answer. Help comes from the God who watches over you through every moment of your day and night. As you pray Psalm 121, be glad for your attentive God.

Psalm 121:1–4 NKJV

I will lift up my eyes to the hills—from whence comes my help? My help comes from the Lord, who made heaven and earth. He will not allow your foot to be moved; He who keeps you will not slumber. Behold, He who keeps Israel shall neither slumber nor sleep.

You are my source of help. You always . . .

You never . . .

Psalm 121:5–8 NKJV

The Lord is your keeper; the Lord is your shade at your right hand. The sun shall not strike you by day, nor the moon by night. The Lord shall preserve you from all evil; He shall preserve your soul. The Lord shall preserve your going out and your coming in from this time forth, and even forevermore.

Keep me from the threats I feel by day and by night. Preserve me today from . . .

Guard my future from . . .

_____

_____

_____

Reflect + Pray + Discuss

1. How do you prepare your heart to worship?

2. When do you worship most fully? Why?

3. What worries do you need to give to God right now to feel free to worship him?

15

God's Dwelling

Old Testament saints who wanted to feel the awe of God's most intense presence had to go to Jerusalem—especially to the temple. For the true believer, there was no better place to be. But Jesus makes it possible for you to draw close to God anywhere and at any time (Hebrews 10:19–22), and the Holy Spirit now makes you a living temple (1 Corinthians 6:19). As you're on the move throughout your day, he accompanies you wherever you go. But as you set aside specific time to converse with God, it is as if you are entering the holy grounds of that monumental stone temple in Jerusalem. As you pray Psalm 84, focus on how you deliberately enter his presence.

Psalm 84:1–2 NIV

> How lovely is your dwelling place, Lord Almighty! My soul yearns, even faints, for the courts of the Lord; my heart and my flesh cry out for the living God.

I'm approaching you . . .

_____

_____

_____

_____

I want . . .

_____

_____

_____

_____

Psalm 84:3–4 NIV

Even the sparrow has found a home, and the swallow a nest for herself, where she may have her young—a place near your altar, Lord Almighty, my King and my God. Blessed are those who dwell in your house; they are ever praising you.

I need you when I feel small and insignificant. When I come close . . .

_____

_____

_____

_____

Even as I worship you, I receive your blessing. You . . .

_____

_____

_____

_____

Psalm 84:5–7 NIV

Blessed are those whose strength is in you, whose hearts are set on pilgrimage As they pass through the Valley of Baka, they make it a place of springs; the autumn rains also cover it with pools. They go from strength to strength, till each appears before God in Zion.

I've had to walk through dry places to get here. I . . .

_____

_____

_____

_____

When I feel dry, you . . .

_____

_____

_____

_____

_____

Psalm 84:8–9 NIV

Hear my prayer, Lord God Almighty; listen to me, God of Jacob. Look on our shield, O God; look with favor on your anointed one.

I'm confident you hear my prayers. Listen when I say . . .

_____

_____

_____

_____

I need your protection . . .

_____

_____

_____

_____

Psalm 84:10 NIV

Better is one day in your courts than a thousand elsewhere; I would rather be a doorkeeper in the house of my God than dwell in the tents of the wicked.

I would rather be near you than anywhere else. You . . .

_____

_____

_____

I prefer your presence to hanging out with people who hate you. I choose to flee . . .

Psalm 84:11–12 NIV

For the Lord God is a sun and shield; the Lord bestows favor and honor; no good thing does he withhold from those whose walk is blameless. Lord Almighty, blessed is the one who trusts in you.

You never withhold your blessings from me. Thank you for . . .

I'm determined to trust you as I go back to life. Help me . . .

Reflect + Pray + Discuss

1. What keeps you from taking time to consciously enter God's presence?

2. What are you looking for when you draw near to God? Is your time about you—or about him?

3. Are you convinced that God's presence is the best place to be? Why—or why not?

16

God's Rescue

God never promised to fix every problem of life. But that doesn't mean he will never rock your world with an astounding rescue you never saw coming. God often intervenes in near-tragic moments. He puts a stop to chronic evil. He eases everyday struggles. And he transforms people who seem dead set against him. Some scholars argue that Psalm 91 was written by Moses, the leader of God's Old Testament people and author of the similar Psalm 90. Just as Moses experienced the Lord's rescue at specific and spectacular moments (Exodus 14:19–20, 16:1–5, and many more), you will witness God act on your behalf at the times and in the places and ways he chooses. As you pray Psalm 91, give thanks to God for his ability to step into your world and save you.

Psalm 91:1–2 ESV

He who dwells in the shelter of the Most High will abide in the shadow of the Almighty. I will say to the Lord, "My refuge and my fortress, my God, in whom I trust."

Your presence is my protection. I will . . .

_____

_____

_____

You are . . .

_____

_____

_____

Psalm 91:3–8 ESV

For he will deliver you from the snare of the fowler and from the deadly pestilence. He will cover you with his pinions, and under his wings you will find refuge; his faithfulness is a shield and buckler. You will not fear the terror of the night, nor the arrow that flies by day, nor the pestilence that stalks in darkness, nor the destruction that wastes at noonday. A thousand may fall at your side, ten thousand at your right hand, but it will not come near you. You will only look with your eyes and see the recompense of the wicked.

I've seen disaster . . .

_____

_____

_____

_____

I know you've rescued me from . . .

_____

_____

_____

_____

Psalm 91:9–13 ESV

Because you have made the Lord your dwelling place—the Most High, who is my refuge—no evil shall be allowed to befall you, no plague come near your tent. For he will command his angels concerning you to guard you in all your ways. On their hands they will bear you up, lest you strike your foot against a stone. You will tread on the lion and the adder; the young lion and the serpent you will trample underfoot.

I need your protection from . . .

_____

_____

_____

I believe you're powerful enough to . . .

Psalm 91:14–16 ESV

"Because he holds fast to me in love, I will deliver him;
I will protect him, because he knows my name. When
he calls to me, I will answer him; I will be with him in
trouble; I will rescue him and honor him. With long life I
will satisfy him and show him my salvation."

I promise to hold fast to you. I will . . .

I'm calling out to you. Answer . . .

Reflect + Pray + Discuss

1. When have you experienced the kind of protection described in this ancient song?

2. When have you desperately prayed and felt God didn't meet your need?

3. How do you balance your confidence in God's ability to rescue you with the truth that he sometimes uses difficult circumstances to grow you or has other purposes beyond your understanding?

Live Freely and Lightly

The religious leaders of Jesus' day made following God an overwhelming load. As Jesus said, "They make strict rules and try to force people to obey them, but they are unwilling to help those who struggle under the weight of their rules" (Matthew 23:4 NCV). God does command your obedience. He will endlessly urge you to conform to his will. But his goal is to lead you into a relationship even more loving and life-giving than anything you can experience with a human being. As you pray Matthew 11, remember that the "yoke" he uses to steer you is easy, and any load he puts on you is light (Matthew 11:30 NIV).

Matthew 11:25–26 MSG

Abruptly Jesus broke into prayer: "Thank you, Father, Lord of heaven and earth. You've concealed your ways from sophisticates and know-it-alls, but spelled them out clearly to ordinary people. Yes, Father, that's the way you like to work."

I'm weighed down by some of the things people say about you—like . . .

_____

_____

_____

_____

I'm doing my best to follow you, but I'm confused about . . .

_____

_____

_____

_____

Matthew 11:27 MSG

Jesus resumed talking to the people, but now tenderly. "The Father has given me all these things to do and say. This is a unique Father-Son operation, coming out of Father and Son intimacies and knowledge. No one knows the Son the way the Father does, nor the Father the way the Son does. But I'm not keeping it to myself; I'm ready to go over it line by line with anyone willing to listen."

Speak tenderly to me. Sometimes I hear a harsh voice when you expect me to . . .

I'm willing to listen. I . . .

Matthew 11:28 MSG

"Are you tired? Worn out? Burned out on religion? Come to me. Get away with me and you'll recover your life. I'll show you how to take a real rest. Walk with me and work with me—watch how I do it. Learn the unforced rhythms of grace. I won't lay anything heavy or ill-fitting on you. Keep company with me and you'll learn to live freely and lightly."

I want to recover my life. I'll get away with you . . .

I need to learn your rhythms of grace. Teach me . . .

_____

_____

_____

Reflect + Pray + Discuss

1. What does it mean to "live freely and lightly" with Jesus?

2. When does following Jesus feel like an unbearable weight? Do those demands come from Jesus—or some other voice?

3. What's your plan to "learn the unforced rhythms of grace"?

Right-Sized Burdens

You know people who expect you to carry their load, slackers who never run out of ways to shift onto you everything from work assignments to emotional baggage. You also know others with true needs, maybe far more than you could ever meet as you struggle with your own responsibilities. Paul offers wisdom on managing these competing demands. He explains that we should carry each other's "burdens" (Galatians 6:2), a word that denotes a boulder too large for any one person to lift. Yet we are each accountable for carrying our own "load" (Galatians 6:5), the word for a Roman soldier's day pack. As you pray Galatians 6, ask God for wisdom to know the difference between burdens that take a group effort to lift and the loads that rightly belong to you or to other individuals.

Galatians 6:1–2 NIV

> Brothers and sisters, if someone is caught in a sin, you who live by the Spirit should restore that person gently.

But watch yourselves, or you also may be tempted. Carry each other's burdens, and in this way you will fulfill the law of Christ.

People are trapped in sin all around me. Show me the right way to . . .

I need strength to help carry other people's burdens. Help me . . .

Galatians 6:3–6 NIV

If anyone thinks they are something when they are not, they deceive themselves. Each one should test their own actions. Then they can take pride in themselves alone, without comparing themselves to someone else, for each one should carry their own load. Nevertheless, the one who receives instruction in the word should share all good things with their instructor.

Show me when I'm not carrying my own weight. I'm responsible for . . .

_____

_____

_____

Help me guard against people who want to abuse me. Teach me . . .

_____

_____

_____

Galatians 6:7–10 NIV

Do not be deceived: God cannot be mocked. A man reaps what he sows. Whoever sows to please their flesh, from the flesh will reap destruction; whoever sows to please the Spirit, from the Spirit will reap eternal life. Let us not become weary in doing good, for at the proper time we will reap a harvest if we do not give up. Therefore, as we have opportunity, let us do good to all people, especially to those who belong to the family of believers.

I can't mock you. I will plant to please your Spirit by . . .

_____

_____

_____

I don't want to become weary doing good. I promise to . . .

Reflect + Pray + Discuss

1. What loads do you carry for others that they need to lift for themselves?

2. What overwhelming weights have you excused yourself from helping others lift?

3. How do you know when you should shoulder a burden yourself—and when you should ask for help?

19

Hebrews 4

Find Rest

God plans for human beings to experience deep rest, but disobedience always takes us far from his peace. The Lord wanted his Old Testament people to find calm in the land he promised to Abraham (Genesis 12:1–7). But when their lack of trust caused them to reject his command to enter the land, he forced them into the desert for the next forty years. They were sentenced to wander until every rebellious adult fell in the sand (Numbers 14:23, 33). Defiance is always costly, causing us to miss God's best. While ultimate rest awaits you in heaven, God wants you to enter his peace right now by following his lead and keeping his commands. As you pray Hebrews 4, ask God to show you the connection between obeying his commands and enjoying his rest.

Hebrews 4:9–11 NLT

So there is a special rest still waiting for the people of God. For all who have entered into God's rest have rested from their labors, just as God did after creating the world. So let us do our best to enter that rest. But if we disobey God, as the people of Israel did, we will fall.

I barely understand what "rest" really means. Show me . . .

My disobedience keeps me from experiencing your rest. I admit . . .

Hebrews 4:12–13 NLT

For the word of God is alive and powerful. It is sharper than the sharpest two-edged sword, cutting between soul and spirit, between joint and marrow. It exposes our innermost thoughts and desires. Nothing in all creation is hidden from God. Everything is naked and exposed before his eyes, and he is the one to whom we are accountable.

I fear the penetrating scalpel of your Word. But I need . . .

My life and my soul lie naked before you. I feel . . .

_____

_____

_____

Hebrews 4:14–16 NLT

So then, since we have a great High Priest who has entered heaven, Jesus the Son of God, let us hold firmly to
what we believe. This High Priest of ours understands our
weaknesses, for he faced all of the same testings we do,
yet he did not sin. So let us come boldly to the throne of
our gracious God. There we will receive his mercy, and
we will find grace to help us when we need it most.

*Great High Priest, you understand my weaknesses. You en-
dured the same tests I do. Teach me the secret of . . .*

_____

_____

_____

*Because of your mercy, I dare approach your throne boldly. I
need your mercy for . . .*

_____

_____

_____

_____

Reflect + Pray + Discuss

1. What keeps you from revealing your whole self to God?

2. How do you allow God's Word to penetrate your life? How do you try to keep it at a safe distance?

3. What steps do you need to take today to enter God's rest?

20

Freedom in Jesus

God has set Christians free. Old Testament believers were subject to countless laws regulating everything from proper sacrifices at the temple to diet and circumcision (Galatians 5:1–12). Not only did Jesus do away with these external religious dictates (Hebrews 10:1–14), but the forgiveness he won on the cross also liberates you from the impossible burden of keeping rules to merit God's approval (Galatians 2:16). The temptation is to use your new freedom to indulge what the Bible calls your "flesh," your fallible and sinful self. God has instead set you free to be remade by his Spirit from the inside out. As you pray Galatians 5, make up your mind to use your freedom for good.

Galatians 5:13–15 NIV

> You, my brothers and sisters, were called to be free. But do not use your freedom to indulge the flesh; rather, serve one another humbly in love. For the entire law is fulfilled

91

in keeping this one command: "Love your neighbor as yourself." If you bite and devour each other, watch out or you will be destroyed by each other.

You set me free to . . .

_____

_____

_____

Destruction happens when I . . .

_____

_____

_____

Galatians 5:16–18 NIV

So I say, walk by the Spirit, and you will not gratify the desires of the flesh. For the flesh desires what is contrary to the Spirit, and the Spirit what is contrary to the flesh. They are in conflict with each other, so that you are not to do whatever you want. But if you are led by the Spirit, you are not under the law.

My flesh wants . . .

_____

_____

_____

Your Spirit . . .

Galatians 5:19–21 NIV

The acts of the flesh are obvious: sexual immorality, impurity and debauchery; idolatry and witchcraft; hatred, discord, jealousy, fits of rage, selfish ambition, dissensions, factions and envy; drunkenness, orgies, and the like. I warn you, as I did before, that those who live like this will not inherit the kingdom of God.

My flesh sometimes controls me. I confess . . .

My sins . . .

Galatians 5:22–25 NIV

But the fruit of the Spirit is love, joy, peace, forbearance, kindness, goodness, faithfulness, gentleness and self-control. Against such things there is no law. Those who belong to Christ Jesus have crucified the flesh with its passions and desires. Since we live by the Spirit, let us keep in step with the Spirit.

Because I belong to Christ, I'm done with . . .

_____

_____

_____

Grow your Spirit's fruit in me. I need . . .

_____

_____

_____

Reflect + Pray + Discuss

1. What does it matter that you are free in Christ?

2. Where do you see the Holy Spirit at work in you?

3. How do you "keep in step with the Spirit"?

The Narrow Way

Jesus told the crowds to "enter through the narrow gate" (Matthew 7:13 NIV). Only a few find the path that leads to life, while most speed down the broad highway to destruction. They assume that one way to God is as good as the next, and the routes that won't make them break a sweat are the best of all. But Jesus warns of false teachers and their deceptive promises. Rather than pointing out the correct way to God, they seek only to exploit you. Beware of their well-rehearsed performances, and look instead for leaders of proven character. Most of all, study and put into practice Jesus' own words. They ground you in him so you can't be shaken. As you pray Matthew 7, recommit yourself to Jesus your Rock.

Matthew 7:13–14 MSG

"Don't look for shortcuts to God. The market is flooded with surefire, easygoing formulas for a successful life that can be practiced in your spare time. Don't fall for that stuff, even though crowds of people do. The way to life—to God!—is vigorous and requires total attention."

Shortcuts to you . . .

_____

_____

_____

_____

My quest for you deserves my total attention. I will . . .

_____

_____

_____

_____

Matthew 7:15–20 MSG

"Be wary of false preachers who smile a lot, dripping with practiced sincerity. Chances are they are out to rip you off some way or other. Don't be impressed with charisma; look for character. Who preachers *are* is the main thing, not what they say. A genuine leader will never exploit your emotions or your pocketbook. These diseased trees with their bad apples are going to be chopped down and burned."

False preachers . . .

_____

_____

_____

_____

Real spiritual leaders . . .

_____

_____

_____

_____

Matthew 7:24–25 MSG

"These words I speak to you are not incidental additions to your life, homeowner improvements to your standard of living. They are foundational words, words to build a life on. If you work these words into your life, you are like a smart carpenter who built his house on solid rock. Rain poured down, the river flooded, a tornado hit—but nothing moved that house. It was fixed to the rock."

Your words are . . .

_____

_____

_____

_____

Building my life on you . . .

_____

_____

_____

_____

Matthew 7:26–27 MSG

"But if you just use my words in Bible studies and don't work them into your life, you are like a stupid carpenter who built his house on the sandy beach. When a storm rolled in and the waves came up, it collapsed like a house of cards."

I don't always work your words into my life. Forgive me for . . .

_____

_____

_____

_____

Warn me when I try to stand in life's storms without you. I need . . .

_____

_____

_____

_____

Reflect + Pray + Discuss

1. When have you been deceived by someone you trusted as a spiritual leader? How did you find your way back to reality?

2. Do you believe that the way to God is "vigorous and requires total attention"? Why—or why not?

3. Why is it wise to act on Jesus' own words?

22

Live Into Love

The apostle Paul had just explained that God makes Christians alive in Christ (Ephesians 2:1–10). He noted that God aims to bring together people once regarded as enemies (Ephesians 2:11–18). He mentions that Christians are a holy temple with Jesus as the cornerstone (Ephesians 2:19–22) and that God has a plan to use the church to reveal his wisdom to the entire universe (Ephesians 3:1–13). And then he says, "When I think of all this, I fall to my knees and pray to the Father" (Ephesians 3:14 NLT). Paul offers up a phenomenal set of requests on behalf of the Ephesians. If he were here today, he would pray that you too would live into God's extraordinary love. As you pray Ephesians 3, speak his words for yourself, your loved ones, and your world.

Ephesians 3:14–16 NLT

> When I think of all this, I fall to my knees and pray to the Father, the Creator of everything in heaven and on earth.

I pray that from his glorious, unlimited resources he will empower you with inner strength through his Spirit.

I fall to my knees . . .

Use your glorious, unlimited resources to . . .

Ephesians 3:17–19 NLT

Then Christ will make his home in your hearts as you trust in him. Your roots will grow down into God's love and keep you strong. And may you have the power to understand, as all God's people should, how wide, how long, how high, and how deep his love is. May you experience the love of Christ, though it is too great to understand fully. Then you will be made complete with all the fullness of life and power that comes from God.

I need to understand . . .

I want to experience . . .

_____

_____

_____

I'm asking for these things so that . . .

_____

_____

_____

Ephesians 3:20–21 NLT

> Now all glory to God, who is able, through his mighty power at work within us, to accomplish infinitely more than we might ask or think. Glory to him in the church and in Christ Jesus through all generations forever and ever! Amen.

I plead with you to accomplish . . .

_____

_____

_____

You deserve praise for . . .

_____

_____

_____

Reflect + Pray + Discuss

1. Is Paul's vision of God's love beyond what you should realistically expect to experience? Why—or why not?

2. What part of this prayer most moves you? Why?

3. How does God accomplish "infinitely more than we might ask or think"? What might that look like in your life?

Become New

Smallness of vision might trap you in a life far less than what God intends. Ephesians 4 details some of the real-life changes God plans to accomplish in you. He aims for you to escape harmful habits and leave the worst parts of yourself behind. He wants to remake your mind and heart and lead you to better actions. But this transformation only happens if you let God diagnose your true condition. Like a doctor who thoroughly tests and evaluates you to uncover a deadly illness, the Lord knows your needs and understands what it takes to make you whole. Open yourself up to what God wants to say to you. As you pray Ephesians 4, invite him to make you new.

Ephesians 4:17–19 NCV

In the Lord's name, I tell you this. Do not continue living like those who do not believe. Their thoughts are worth nothing. They do not understand, and they know nothing, because they refuse to listen. So they cannot have the life that God gives. They have lost all feeling of shame, and they use their lives for doing evil. They continually want to do all kinds of evil.

I sometimes think and act like I don't believe. I . . .

I promise not to shut out your voice when . . .

Ephesians 4:20–24 NCV

But what you learned in Christ was not like this. I know that you heard about him, and you are in him, so you were taught the truth that is in Jesus. You were taught to leave your old self—to stop living the evil way you lived before. That old self becomes worse, because people are fooled by the evil things they want to do. But you were taught to be made new in your hearts, to become a new person. That new person is made to be like God—made to be truly good and holy.

Don't let me be fooled by . . .

_____

_____

_____

_____

I'll leave behind . . .

_____

_____

_____

Make me . . .

_____

_____

_____

Ephesians 4:25–28 NCV

So you must stop telling lies. Tell each other the truth, because we all belong to each other in the same body. When you are angry, do not sin, and be sure to stop being angry before the end of the day. Do not give the devil a way to defeat you. Those who are stealing must stop stealing and start working. They should earn an honest living for themselves. Then they will have something to share with those who are poor.

Show me exactly what you want to change in me. Help me see . . .

Confront me when I'm less than honest about . . .

Reflect + Pray + Discuss

1. How are you a changed person because you follow Jesus?

2. What parts of your life still need to be made whole?

3. How does unresolved anger lead to defeat?

24

Grow Up

The new life that God begins in you grows up and up. There's no limit to what the Lord wants to do in and through you. He declares that "Whoever is a believer in Christ is a new creation. The old way of living has disappeared. A new way of living has come into existence" (2 Corinthians 5:17 GW). But it takes a lifetime and beyond for the new you to fully emerge. In Ephesians 4 God continues to address the specific changes he plans to make in you. He fills your mouth with uplifting words. He calms your anger. And he shows love to you so that you can spread it to others. As you continue to pray Ephesians 4, ask God to keep you on an upward path.

Ephesians 4:29 NCV

> When you talk, do not say harmful things, but say what people need—words that will help others become stronger. Then what you say will do good to those who listen to you.

My words are . . .

_____

_____

_____

_____

I want my words to . . .

_____

_____

_____

_____

Ephesians 4:30–32 NCV

And do not make the Holy Spirit sad. The Spirit is God's proof that you belong to him. God gave you the Spirit to show that God will make you free when the final day comes. Do not be bitter or angry or mad. Never shout angrily or say things to hurt others. Never do anything evil. Be kind and loving to each other, and forgive each other just as God forgave you in Christ.

Calm my feelings toward . . .

_____

_____

_____

_____

Because you have forgiven me, I will . . .

Ephesians 5:1–2 NCV

You are God's children whom he loves, so try to be like him. Live a life of love just as Christ loved us and gave himself for us as a sweet-smelling offering and sacrifice to God.

I need your help to reflect your love to . . .

You sacrificed yourself for me, so I will . . .

110

Reflect + Pray + Discuss

1. How can you build a habit of speaking words that lift up others?

2. How does God's love for you empower you to love people?

3. Is it reasonable for God to expect you to sacrifice like Jesus did? Why—or why not?

Find Peace

"You will keep in perfect peace those whose minds are steadfast," wrote the prophet Isaiah, "because they trust in you" (Isaiah 26:3 NIV). Jesus said, "Peace I leave with you; my peace I give you. I do not give to you as the world gives. Do not let your hearts be troubled and do not be afraid" (John 14:27 NIV). The apostle Paul wrote, "To be spiritually minded is life and peace" (Romans 8:6 NKJV). And in his brief letter to his close friends in the city of Philippi, Paul explains how this peace permeates your mind. By unburdening yourself through prayer and filling your thoughts with things worthy of admiration, you will experience God's calm. As you pray Philippians 4, let God transform your mind and lead you to peace.

Philippians 4:6–7 NLT

> Don't worry about anything; instead, pray about everything. Tell God what you need, and thank him for all he

has done. Then you will experience God's peace, which exceeds anything we can understand. His peace will guard your hearts and minds as you live in Christ Jesus.

My mind overflows with worry. I need . . .

_____

_____

_____

_____

_____

I'm grateful for . . .

_____

_____

_____

_____

_____

Philippians 4:8–9 NLT

And now, dear brothers and sisters, one final thing. Fix your thoughts on what is true, and honorable, and right, and pure, and lovely, and admirable. Think about things that are excellent and worthy of praise. Keep putting into practice all you learned and received from me—everything you heard from me and saw me doing. Then the God of peace will be with you.

Some of my thoughts spoil your peace. I need to stop thinking about . . .

_____

_____

_____

I'm determined to focus on . . .

_____

_____

_____

Reflect + Pray + Discuss

1. What do you expect the experience of God's peace to be like?

2. When have you tried to trust God with your worries— and you still felt anxious? How did you press on?

3. How does praying with others and getting their encouragement help you find peace—or not?

Be Content

Philippians is the Bible's book of joy, with the word appearing more than a dozen times as a noun or verb in four short chapters. But even a quick read of the book shows that the apostle Paul finds joy in unexpected places. He writes an upbeat letter despite the fact that he is in chains for his faith. He rejoices that his imprisonment has caused the news about Jesus to spread. And he isn't upset by people on the outside who are trying to make trouble for him (Philippians 1:12–18). His story shows the secret of contentment in any situation, proof that happiness depends less on making your circumstances comfortable than on maintaining your connection to God. As you pray Philippians 4, ask the Lord to teach you this crucial lesson.

Philippians 4:10–12 NLT

> How I praise the Lord that you are concerned about me again. I know you have always been concerned for me,

but you didn't have the chance to help me. Not that I was ever in need, for I have learned how to be content with whatever I have. I know how to live on almost nothing or with everything. I have learned the secret of living in every situation, whether it is with a full stomach or empty, with plenty or little.

I admit it. I'm frustrated by . . .

Train me to have a new attitude of . . .

Philippians 4:13–14 NLT

For I can do everything through Christ, who gives me strength. Even so, you have done well to share with me in my present difficulty.

On my own I'm not strong enough for life. I . . .

Because of your strength inside me I can . . .

Reflect + Pray + Discuss

1. When have you felt most content—and the most discontent? What would Paul say to you about that?

2. How would you react if you suddenly lost everything?

3. How does God give you strength?

27

Seek God

Jesus knows how easily daily realities overshadow our best spiritual intentions. Whether you possess much or suffer lack, thoughts about what you want, need, and buy can become all-consuming (Matthew 6:24). Building security and wealth can become a calamitous distraction (1 Timothy 6:5–10, 17–19). Jesus reminds you that your heavenly Father watches over your life. If he clothes flowers with grandeur and ensures that the smallest birds have enough to eat, he will surely supply your true needs. He invites you to let go of worry and count on his provision, and he commands you to seek him and his reign above any possession. As you pray Matthew 6, trust God to meet your material needs.

Matthew 6:25–27 NKJV

"Therefore I say to you, do not worry about your life, what you will eat or what you will drink; nor about your body, what you will put on. Is not life more than food and the body more than clothing? Look at the birds of the air, for they neither sow nor reap nor gather into barns; yet your heavenly Father feeds them. Are you not of more value than they? Which of you by worrying can add one cubit to his stature?"

I worry about . . .

_____

_____

_____

_____

My life is bigger than . . .

_____

_____

_____

_____

Matthew 6:28–30 NKJV

"So why do you worry about clothing? Consider the lilies of the field, how they grow: they neither toil nor spin; and yet I say to you that even Solomon in all his glory was not arrayed like one of these. Now if God so clothes the grass of the field, which today is, and tomorrow is thrown into the oven, will He not much more clothe you, O you of little faith?"

You show your care . . .

_____

_____

_____

_____

Thank you for . . .

_____

_____

_____

_____

Matthew 6:31–34 NKJV

"Therefore do not worry, saying, 'What shall we eat?' or 'What shall we drink?' or 'What shall we wear?' For after all these things the Gentiles seek. For your heavenly Father knows that you need all these things. But seek first the kingdom of God and His righteousness, and all these things shall be added to you. Therefore do not worry about tomorrow, for tomorrow will worry about its own things. Sufficient for the day is its own trouble."

I trust you to . . .

_____

_____

_____

I will make you my highest priority by . . .

_____

_____

_____

Reflect + Pray + Discuss

1. Does working hard make it harder or easier to trust God to supply your needs?

2. What most concerns you about living out these words?

3. How do you "seek first the kingdom of God and His righteousness"?

28

Take Delight

Many people who do evil look like they have it made. As one ancient songwriter put it, "They suffer no pain. Their bodies are healthy. They have no drudgery in their lives like ordinary people. They are not plagued with problems like others" (Psalm 73:4–5 GW). Their success causes them to "wear arrogance like a necklace" (Psalm 73:6 GW). God cautions against envying people who sin without worrying about consequences. He instructs you to quit eyeing their success and put your focus on him. When you make God your highest happiness, he will give you more and more of himself. He will vindicate you in plain sight of people who think you're stupid to follow him. As you pray Psalm 37, put your hope in God.

Psalm 37:1–2 NIV

> Do not fret because of those who are evil or be envious of those who do wrong; for like the grass they will soon wither, like green plants they will soon die away.

I'm envious when I see . . .

The success enjoyed by people who do wrong can't last. They will . . .

Psalm 37:3–6 NIV

Trust in the Lord and do good; dwell in the land and enjoy safe pasture. Take delight in the Lord, and he will give you the desires of your heart. Commit your way to the Lord; trust in him and he will do this: he will make your righteous reward shine like the dawn, your vindication like the noonday sun.

I demonstrate my trust in you by . . .

I count on you to . . .

_____

_____

_____

_____

Psalm 37:7–9 NIV

Be still before the Lord and wait patiently for him; do not fret when people succeed in their ways, when they carry out their wicked schemes. Refrain from anger and turn from wrath; do not fret—it leads only to evil. For those who are evil will be destroyed, but those who hope in the Lord will inherit the land.

I wait patiently for . . .

_____

_____

_____

_____

Because I hope in you . . .

_____

_____

_____

_____

Reflect + Pray + Discuss

1. When has watching evil people succeed tempted you toward doing wrong?

2. What does this passage teach you about trusting God?

3. What do you expect of God if you "take delight" in him?

29

Psalm 19

See God

God designed the world as a showcase of his glory. His creation tells the story of who he is. His handiwork clearly declares his divine power and character, leaving people without excuse when they ignore him (Romans 1:20). But God's revelation of himself doesn't end with the natural world. He also reveals himself through his words. He has been speaking since humankind's earliest days (Genesis 2:15–17). His law disclosed his goodness (Psalm 119:7). His prophets announced his plans (Hebrews 1:1). And all of Scripture explains how people should live. Second Timothy 3:16 says, "Every part of Scripture is God-breathed and useful one way or another— showing us truth, exposing our rebellion, correcting our mistakes, training us to live God's way" (MSG). As you pray Psalm 19, look for God's revelation of himself in his works and in his words.

Psalm 19:1–4 NCV

The heavens declare the glory of God, and the skies announce what his hands have made. Day after day they tell the story; night after night they tell it again. They have no speech or words; they have no voice to be heard. But their message goes out through all the world; their words go everywhere on earth.

When I study your creation . . .

Your message . . .

Psalm 19:7–8 NCV

The teachings of the Lord are perfect; they give new strength. The rules of the Lord can be trusted; they make plain people wise. The orders of the Lord are right; they make people happy. The commands of the Lord are pure; they light up the way.

Your teachings are . . .

_____

_____

_____

Through your commands I learn . . .

_____

_____

_____

Reflect + Pray + Discuss

1. How do you see God most clearly—through his works or his words?

2. What do God's words teach you that his works do not?

3. If you knew nothing about Jesus, what would you understand about God?

Meet God

When Jesus stepped into the world's darkness, he allowed humankind to meet God face-to-face. Since earth's beginning, the Lord had shown himself through his works and his words, but human understanding of him remained shadowy. So Jesus arrived to let God's glory shine on earth (John 1:14). Born in the town of Bethlehem (Luke 2:4–7), he was no ordinary human child. He was "the Word" who had existed from all eternity . . . had always been in relationship with God . . . and in fact was God himself (John 1:1). He left the splendor of heaven and took on human flesh, giving all people the opportunity to accept or reject him (John 1:12). As you pray John 1, be prepared to meet God.

John 1:1–5 ESV

> In the beginning was the Word, and the Word was with God, and the Word was God. He was in the beginning with God. All things were made through him, and without

him was not any thing made that was made. In him was life, and the life was the light of men. The light shines in the darkness, and the darkness has not overcome it.

Jesus, you are . . .

You brought . . .

John 1:9–13 ESV

The true light, which gives light to everyone, was coming into the world. He was in the world, and the world was made through him, yet the world did not know him. He came to his own, and his own people did not receive him. But to all who did receive him, who believed in his name, he gave the right to become children of God, who were born, not of blood nor of the will of the flesh nor of the will of man, but of God.

Some who see you . . .

_____

_____

_____

When I meet you . . .

_____

_____

_____

John 1:14 ESV

> And the Word became flesh and dwelt among us, and
> we have seen his glory, glory as of the only Son from the
> Father, full of grace and truth.

Because you dared to live as a human being . . .

_____

_____

_____

Your grace and truth . . .

_____

_____

_____

Reflect + Pray + Discuss

1. What do you know about God because Jesus came and lived in this world?

2. Does it matter if Jesus is actually God? Why—or why not?

3. What does it mean to "receive" Jesus?

The Olive Press

Hours before his crucifixion, Jesus knelt to pray. He returned to a garden just east of Jerusalem where he had often gone with his followers—Gethsemane, meaning "Olive Press." As Jesus looked ahead to his death, he pleaded with his Father to reveal another way to cleanse your sins and the sins of all humankind. "My Father, if it is possible," he prayed, "may this cup be taken from me. Yet not as I will, but as you will" (Matthew 26:39 NIV). In anguish his sweat "became like great drops of blood falling down to the ground" (Luke 22:44 ESV). When it was clear that there was no way around the suffering that lay before him, he surrendered himself to his Father's plan. As you pray Matthew 26, know that Jesus went willingly to the cross for you.

Matthew 26:36–38 NIV

> Then Jesus went with his disciples to a place called Geth-semane, and he said to them, "Sit here while I go over there

and pray." He took Peter and the two sons of Zebedee along with him, and he began to be sorrowful and troubled. Then he said to them, "My soul is overwhelmed with sorrow to the point of death. Stay here and keep watch with me."

You went to the garden . . .

_____

_____

_____

You felt . . .

_____

_____

_____

Matthew 26:39–44 NIV

Going a little farther, he fell with his face to the ground and prayed, "My Father, if it is possible, may this cup be taken from me. Yet not as I will, but as you will." Then he returned to his disciples and found them sleeping. "Couldn't you men keep watch with me for one hour?" he asked Peter. "Watch and pray so that you will not fall into temptation. The spirit is willing, but the flesh is weak." He went away a second time and prayed, "My Father, if it is not possible for this cup to be taken away unless I drink it, may your will be done." When he came back, he again found them sleeping, because their eyes were heavy. So he left them and went away once more and prayed the third time, saying the same thing.

Your disciples . . .

_____

_____

_____

_____

You pleaded . . .

_____

_____

_____

_____

You decided . . .

_____

_____

_____

_____

Matthew 26:45–46 NIV

Then he returned to the disciples and said to them, "Are you still sleeping and resting? Look, the hour has come, and the Son of Man is delivered into the hands of sinners. Rise! Let us go! Here comes my betrayer!"

Don't let me doze while you . . .

_____

_____

_____

I surrender . . .

_____

_____

_____

Reflect + Pray + Discuss

1. How would you have reacted had you accompanied Jesus to Gethsemane?

2. Did Jesus go to the cross grudgingly—or not? How do you know? Why does that matter to you today?

3. In what areas of life is God asking you to surrender to him?

32

Jesus Dies

The prophet Isaiah predicted that God's chosen one would suffer on your behalf. Hundreds of years before Jesus died, the prophet proclaimed, "He was wounded for our rebellious acts. He was crushed for our sins. He was punished so that we could have peace, and we received healing from his wounds" (Isaiah 53:5 GW). The New Testament account of Jesus' death no doubt impacts your feelings, but it should also move your mind. Search for your place in the story. Are you a criminal . . . a ruler . . . a soldier . . . a face in the crowd . . . a centurion . . . a follower who stood at a distance? Or are you all of those and more? That ancient moment—and your response—matters more than any other in all of history. As you pray Luke 23, ask God for fresh insights into your Savior's death.

Luke 23:32–38 ESV

Two others, who were criminals, were led away to be put to death with him. And when they came to the place that is called The Skull, there they crucified him, and the criminals, one on his right and one on his left. And Jesus said, "Father, forgive them, for they know not what they do." And they cast lots to divide his garments. And the people stood by, watching, but the rulers scoffed at him, saying, "He saved others; let him save himself, if he is the Christ of God, his Chosen One!" The soldiers also mocked him, coming up and offering him sour wine and saying, "If you are the King of the Jews, save yourself!" There was also an inscription over him, "This is the King of the Jews."

Sinful criminals were crucified with you. I . . .

Rulers and soldiers scoffed and mocked. I . . .

Luke 23:39–43 ESV

One of the criminals who were hanged railed at him, saying, "Are you not the Christ? Save yourself and us!" But the other rebuked him, saying, "Do you not fear God, since you are under the same sentence of condemnation? And we indeed justly, for we are receiving the due reward of our deeds; but this man has done nothing wrong." And he said, "Jesus, remember me when you come into your kingdom." And he said to him, "Truly, I say to you, today you will be with me in Paradise."

One criminal ridiculed your claim to be the Messiah. I . . .

You . . .

Luke 23:44–49 ESV

It was now about the sixth hour, and there was darkness over the whole land until the ninth hour, while the sun's light failed. And the curtain of the temple was torn in two. Then Jesus, calling out with a loud voice, said, "Father, into your hands I commit my spirit!" And having said this he breathed his last. Now when the centurion saw what had taken place, he praised God, saying, "Certainly this man was innocent!" And all the crowds that had assembled for this spectacle, when they saw what had taken place, returned home beating their breasts. And all his acquaintances and the women who had followed him from Galilee stood at a distance watching these things.

People who watched you die . . .

_____

_____

_____

Your death . . .

_____

_____

_____

Reflect + Pray + Discuss

1. How much do you think about Christ's sacrifice on the cross—or not? Why?

2. What part would you have played in that scene?

3. What difference will Christ's death make for you today?

Jesus Rises

Jesus plainly told his followers that he would die and come back to life. Mark writes, "Jesus began to teach them that the Son of Man must suffer many things and that he would be rejected by the Jewish elders, the leading priests, and the teachers of the law. He told them that the Son of Man must be killed and then rise from the dead after three days" (Mark 8:31 NCV). But after Jesus rose, even his closest friends were slow to process what had happened. His female followers found their Lord's empty tomb and heard an angel announce that Jesus had risen (Mark 16:4–6). The men thought their report was nonsense and puzzled over what had happened (Luke 24:11). As you pray Mark 16, ask God for a mind and heart quick to believe.

Mark 16:1–3 NCV

> The day after the Sabbath day, Mary Magdalene, Mary the mother of James, and Salome bought some sweet-smelling

spices to put on Jesus' body. Very early on that day, the first day of the week, soon after sunrise, the women were on their way to the tomb. They said to each other, "Who will roll away for us the stone that covers the entrance of the tomb?"

I understand why people would mourn your death. I feel . . .

I sometimes feel helpless. But you . . .

Mark 16:4–7 NCV

Then the women looked and saw that the stone had already been rolled away, even though it was very large. The women entered the tomb and saw a young man wearing a white robe and sitting on the right side, and they were afraid.

But the man said, "Don't be afraid. You are looking for Jesus from Nazareth, who has been crucified. He has risen from the dead; he is not here. Look, here is the place they laid him. Now go and tell his followers and Peter, 'Jesus is going into Galilee ahead of you, and you will see him there as he told you before.'"

I'm afraid when . . .

_____

_____

_____

Your resurrection . . .

_____

_____

_____

Mark 16:8 NCV

The women were confused and shaking with fear, so they left the tomb and ran away. They did not tell anyone about what happened, because they were afraid.

Your surprises can make me shake with fear. I . . .

_____

_____

_____

Clear up my confusion so I can . . .

_____

_____

_____

_____

Reflect + Pray + Discuss

1. When are you slow to believe God? When do you enthusiastically act on his truth?

2. How would you have reacted to the news that Jesus had risen?

3. What difference will Christ's resurrection make for you today?

Saved

The spiritual transformation that occurs in your life demonstrates that Jesus' life, death, and resurrection weren't in vain. Before Jesus was born, an angel announced, "You will name him Jesus [He Saves], because he will save his people from their sins" (Matthew 1:21 GW). Jesus saves you not only from sin's penalty but from its power, and the apostle Paul lays out the results of this salvation in his short letter to Titus, pastor to a rough crowd on the island of Crete (Titus 1:5, 12). Salvation in the real world entails gaining forgiveness . . . entering new life . . . abandoning sin . . . maturing in devotion to God. As you pray Titus 2–3, let God show you what it means to grow up in your salvation.

Titus 2:11–14 NLT

> For the grace of God has been revealed, bringing salvation to all people. And we are instructed to turn from godless living and sinful pleasures. We should live in this evil world

with wisdom, righteousness, and devotion to God, while we look forward with hope to that wonderful day when the glory of our great God and Savior, Jesus Christ, will be revealed. He gave his life to free us from every kind of sin, to cleanse us, and to make us his very own people, totally committed to doing good deeds.

Your grace . . .

_____

_____

_____

Because of your salvation . . .

_____

_____

_____

Jesus gave his life . . .

_____

_____

_____

Titus 3:3 NLT

Once we, too, were foolish and disobedient. We were misled and became slaves to many lusts and pleasures. Our lives were full of evil and envy, and we hated each other.

Without you I . . .

_____

_____

_____

Titus 3:4–8 NLT

But—"When God our Savior revealed his kindness and love, he saved us, not because of the righteous things we had done, but because of his mercy. He washed away our sins, giving us a new birth and new life through the Holy Spirit. He generously poured out the Spirit upon us through Jesus Christ our Savior. Because of his grace he declared us righteous and gave us confidence that we will inherit eternal life." This is a trustworthy saying, and I want you to insist on these teachings so that all who trust in God will devote themselves to doing good. These teachings are good and beneficial for everyone.

You saved me because . . .

_____

_____

_____

You mercifully . . .

_____

_____

_____

This truth is . . .

_____

_____

_____

Reflect + Pray + Discuss

1. What does salvation mean for your life—right here, right now?

2. How much are you living into your salvation—or letting it go to waste?

3. What motivates you to let God save you through and through?

Served

What Jesus accomplished on the cross should move you to serve. At the start of Philippians 2, the apostle Paul asks, "Are you better off because you belong to Christ? Does his love lift you up? Has he brought you into community? Has he given you a new heart?" The grammar embedded in his questions indicates that Paul expects positive answers. Jesus has done all those things and more for his followers. And because those things are true, you are to have the same servant attitude that Jesus displayed on earth (Philippians 2:5). When you can't see beyond yourself to help others, remember that you have a source of unlimited motivation. You can love because God first loved you (1 John 4:19). As you pray Philippians 2, let God remind you of what he has done for you.

Philippians 2:1 NLT

Is there any encouragement from belonging to Christ? Any comfort from his love? Any fellowship together in the Spirit? Are your hearts tender and compassionate?

You've given me . . .

You've made me . . .

Philippians 2:2–4 NLT

Then make me truly happy by agreeing wholeheartedly with each other, loving one another, and working together with one mind and purpose. Don't be selfish; don't try to impress others. Be humble, thinking of others as better than yourselves. Don't look out only for your own interests, but take an interest in others, too.

150

Because of you I will . . .

Train me to . . .

Philippians 2:5–8 NLT

You must have the same attitude that Christ Jesus had. Though he was God, he did not think of equality with God as something to cling to. Instead, he gave up his divine privileges; he took the humble position of a slave and was born as a human being. When he appeared in human form, he humbled himself in obedience to God and died a criminal's death on a cross.

You . . .

I . . .

_____

_____

_____

_____

Philippians 2:9–11 NLT

Therefore, God elevated him to the place of highest honor
and gave him the name above all other names, that at the
name of Jesus every knee should bow, in heaven and on
earth and under the earth, and every tongue confess that
Jesus Christ is Lord, to the glory of God the Father.

I praise you for . . .

_____

_____

_____

_____

Every person . . .

_____

_____

_____

_____

_____

Reflect + Pray + Discuss

1. What has God given you—and done for you—that empowers you to love?

2. What does it mean to have "the same attitude that Christ Jesus had"?

3. Do you bow to Jesus—or not? How?

Sent

Jesus doesn't intend for the truth about himself to be kept secret among Christians. His "Great Commission" in Matthew 28 sending his followers into the world was built on some of God's oldest promises. God told Abraham, "Through you every family on earth will be blessed" (Genesis 12:3 GW). David looked forward to a time when "All the ends of the earth will remember and return to the Lord" (Psalm 22:27 GW). And the Lord said of the coming Savior, "I have also made you a light for the nations so that you would save people all over the world" (Isaiah 49:6 GW). As a follower of Jesus, you have an indispensable role in bringing life to the world. As you pray Matthew 28, ask God to give you his heart for the people he loves.

Matthew 28:18 GW

> When Jesus came near, he spoke to them. He said, "All authority in heaven and on earth has been given to me."

Jesus, come near me and . . .

_____

_____

_____

You possess authority . . .

_____

_____

_____

Matthew 28:19–20 GW

"So wherever you go, make disciples of all nations: Baptize them in the name of the Father, and of the Son, and of the Holy Spirit. Teach them to do everything I have commanded you."

People from every nation . . .

_____

_____

_____

I will . . .

_____

_____

_____

_____

Matthew 28:20 GW

"And remember that I am always with you until the end of time."

Because you will never abandon me, I can . . .

_____

_____

_____

Reflect + Pray + Discuss

1. What do you think of Jesus' command that his followers tell the world about him?

2. How is that task best accomplished?

3. What role do you play in fulfilling this mandate?

Basics

Like the great command to love God and others (Matthew 22:34–40), these words from the prophet Micah bring you back to simple faith. Micah spoke in an era when invaders were about to destroy the Old Testament kingdom of Israel. He denounced God's people for serving false gods and observing an outward religion that left the Lord out of everyday life. God had grown tired of empty words and meaningless sacrifices (Isaiah 1:14–15; Amos 5:21–24). He declared that real obedience far outshines any religious show (1 Samuel 15:22). When your connection with God grows hollow or pretentious, come back to the basic commands of Micah 6:8. As you pray Micah 6, let God renew your authentic faith.

Micah 6:6–7 ESV

"With what shall I come before the Lord, and bow myself before God on high? Shall I come before him with burnt offerings, with calves a year old? Will the Lord be pleased with thousands of rams, with ten thousands of rivers of oil? Shall I give my firstborn for my transgression, the fruit of my body for the sin of my soul?"

I've tried to impress you by . . .

_____

_____

_____

_____

Nothing I bring you . . .

_____

_____

_____

_____

Micah 6:8 ESV

He has told you, O man, what is good; and what does the Lord require of you but to do justice, and to love kindness, and to walk humbly with your God?

You require . . .

_____

_____

_____

_____

You're reminding me . . .

_____

_____

_____

_____

Reflect + Pray + Discuss

1. When has your relationship with God become a tired routine rather than a living reality?

2. What simple commands sum up your life with God?

3. What does it look like in everyday life to do justice . . . love kindness . . . and walk humbly?

38

Isaiah 40

Fresh Strength

Just as the stars of the sky never go missing, God's care for you never ends. The people of Israel—also called Jacob in these words spoken by the prophet Isaiah—complained that God had forgotten them. Their problems seemed too big for him to resolve. Their wretched lives felt beyond his help. God's people wondered aloud if he cared for them at all. But night after night the sweep of the heavens declares the Lord's character and might (Psalm 19:1–6; Romans 1:20). The God who calls the stars by name never forgets you. He will not weary, and he promises his power to everyone who relies on him. As you pray Isaiah 40, let God make you strong for your walk with him.

Isaiah 40:26 GW

> Look at the sky and see. Who created these things? Who brings out the stars one by one? He calls them all by name. Because of the greatness of his might and the strength of his power, not one of them is missing.

Your creation . . .

_____

_____

_____

_____

Your power . . .

_____

_____

_____

_____

Isaiah 40:27–28 GW

Jacob, why do you complain? Israel, why do you say, "My way is hidden from the Lord, and my rights are ignored by my God"? Don't you know? Haven't you heard? The eternal God, the Lord, the Creator of the ends of the earth, doesn't grow tired or become weary. His understanding is beyond reach.

Your care . . .

_____

_____

_____

_____

You never . . .

_____

_____

_____

_____

Isaiah 40:29–31 GW

He gives strength to those who grow tired and increases the strength of those who are weak. Even young people grow tired and become weary, and young men will stumble and fall. Yet, the strength of those who wait with hope in the Lord will be renewed. They will soar on wings like eagles. They will run and won't become weary. They will walk and won't grow tired.

I feel . . .

_____

_____

_____

You . . .

_____

_____

_____

_____

Renew me so I can . . .

Reflect + Pray + Discuss

1. Do you ever doubt God's care? Do you ever question his power? Why—or why not?

2. How do you "wait with hope for the Lord"?

3. What kind of strength do you need right now?

Abide

"These things I have spoken to you," Jesus said, "that my joy may be in you, and that your joy may be full" (John 15:11). He made no secret that he came to give life (John 10:10). But that life is yours only as you stay tightly connected to him. You can't get it from a program or class or conference. It doesn't come from a speaker or song or book. Jesus himself is your fullness. Just as a branch needs a trunk or a stem to survive, you experience abundance as you "abide" in Jesus—a word that means to "dwell" in him, to "stay put," "settle in," or "sink deeper." And you can expect his Father to tend and prune you so you bear maximum fruit. As you pray John 15, look to Jesus as your source of life.

John 15:1–4 ESV

"I am the true vine, and my Father is the vinedresser. Every branch in me that does not bear fruit he takes away, and every branch that does bear fruit he prunes, that it may bear more fruit. Already you are clean because of the word that I have spoken to you. Abide in me, and I in you. As the branch cannot bear fruit by itself, unless it abides in the vine, neither can you, unless you abide in me."

From you I receive . . .

_____

_____

_____

Cut away . . .

_____

_____

_____

John 15:5–6 ESV

"I am the vine; you are the branches. Whoever abides in me and I in him, he it is that bears much fruit, for apart from me you can do nothing. If anyone does not abide in me he is thrown away like a branch and withers; and the branches are gathered, thrown into the fire, and burned."

You are . . .

_____

_____

_____

_____

Without you . . .

_____

_____

_____

Reflect + Pray + Discuss

1. How do you stay tightly connected to Jesus?

2. What kind of life do you experience by abiding in Jesus?

3. When has God pruned you to make you more fruitful?

Bear Fruit

Jesus says that abiding in him will cause you to "bear much fruit" (John 15:8 ESV). By maintaining your connection to him, you won't wither away (John 15:6). You'll pray in line with his words and receive what you ask (John 15:7). You'll spread the care that you get from Jesus (John 15:9, 12). You'll continue to experience the best of his love—obeying his commands, living sacrificially for others, and enjoying close friendship with him (John 15:10, 13, 15). Your existence will be continually filled with joy (John 15:11). And this fruit will prove to the world that you follow Jesus (John 15:8). As you pray John 15, ask God for a life that bears fruit.

John 15:7–11 ESV

"If you abide in me, and my words abide in you, ask whatever you wish, and it will be done for you. By this my Father is glorified, that you bear much fruit and so prove to be my disciples. As the Father has loved me, so have I loved you. Abide in my love. If you keep my commandments, you will abide in my love, just as I have kept my Father's commandments and abide in his love. These things I have spoken to you, that my joy may be in you, and that your joy may be full."

I bring you glory . . .

_____

_____

_____

If I keep your commands . . .

_____

_____

_____

John 15:12–13 ESV

"This is my commandment, that you love one another as I have loved you. Greater love has no one than this, that someone lay down his life for his friends."

Real love . . .

_____

_____

_____

_____

The greatest love . . .

_____

_____

_____

John 15:14–17 ESV

"You are my friends if you do what I command you. No longer do I call you servants, for the servant does not know what his master is doing; but I have called you friends, for all that I have heard from my Father I have made known to you. You did not choose me, but I chose you and appointed you that you should go and bear fruit and that your fruit should abide, so that whatever you ask the Father in my name, he may give it to you. These things I command you, so that you will love one another."

Friendship with you . . .

_____

_____

_____

More than anything I want . . .

_____

_____

_____

Reflect + Pray + Discuss

1. Why bear fruit?

2. What holds you back from a more fruit-filled life?

3. What is your next step in praying the Scriptures?

Kevin Johnson is the creator of the first-of-its-kind *Pray the Scriptures Bible* and the bestselling author or co-author of more than fifty books and Bible products for adults, students, and children. His training includes an MDiv from Fuller Theological Seminary and a BA in English and print journalism from the University of Wisconsin—River Falls. With a background as a youth worker, senior nonfiction book editor, and teaching pastor, he now leads Emmaus Road Church in metro Minneapolis. Kevin is married to Lyn, and they have three almost-grown children.

Learn more at kevinjohnsonbooks.com.

Thousands of Prayers Alongside Full Text of Scripture

Combining both Scripture and prayer in one beautiful package, this Bible is a dynamic quiet time or devotional resource filled with Scripture-specific prayers meant to be read and prayed alongside the verses that inspired them. Approach the throne of grace with confidence as you learn to pray words you know God will want to hear—and how you can apply them to your own life.

Ideal for anyone looking to grow closer to God through their prayers, *Pray the Scriptures Bible* includes these special features:

- more than 4,500 new Scripture-specific prayers
- a guide to praying the Scriptures
- *GOD'S WORD* Translation
- introductions for each book of the Bible
- articles based on major categories of prayer
- index of prayers that appear in Scripture
- topical prayer guide

Pray the Scriptures Bible by Kevin Johnson

BETHANYHOUSE

Stay up-to-date on your favorite books and authors with our *free* e-newsletters. Sign up today at bethanyhouse.com.

Find us on Facebook. facebook.com/bethanyhousepublishers

Follow us on Twitter. @bethany_house